FROM VICTIM
TO VICTOR

DERRICK L. FRAZIER

MOUNTAIN ARBOR PRESS

MOUNTAIN ARBOR
PRESS
Alpharetta, GA

ISBN: 978-1-63183-636-7 - Paperback
eISBN: 978-1-63183-637-4 - ePub
eISBN: 978-1-63183-638-1 - mobi

Printed in the United States of America   0 5 1 4 1 9

⊛This paper meets the requirements of ANSI/NISO Z39.48-1992 (Permanence of Paper)

To my mentor, Mckinely "Fyabird" Lewis

Contents

Foreword

When life puts its hands around your throat and strangles you . . .

When you want to succeed as bad as you want to breathe . . .

You have no choice but to fight—fight for your life and fight for everything that you love. You have no choice but to look up in the sky and thank God for another day. Thank God you survived!

When I was a boy, I thought like a boy, I acted like a boy, but when I became a man, I put away childish things.

What will you do when life throws everything at you and the kitchen sink? Will you die? Will you give up? Or, will you live to fight another day? What are you going to do in your struggle? Are you going to be a **victim, or a victor?**

—*Galen Workcuff*

Acknowledgments

If I were to start off by thanking people before I thanked my Father, protector, and provider, I would be dead wrong. Many people have written me off and many people have abandoned me, but through this journey called life there has been one that has never left me nor forsaken me. If it were not for God's mercy, His abundant grace, and above all, His agape love, I would have been dead a long time ago.

To my wonderful mother, who carried me for nine months and did her best to raise me—I love you. You told me the best way to show you that I was sorry for my actions was to take what you taught me and make something of myself.

To my father, who helped make me—growing up I used to think you hated me. Whether you did or not, I know now that you love me. When you tell me that you love me and that you are proud of me, it means more than what you are saying.

To my foster mother, Joyce Andrews, one of the hardest, most dedicated, strongest single women I know — I appreciate *everything* that you've done for me. You spoke over my life so much, and I thank you. I love you always.

To Mr. McGee, one of the wisest and bravest men I know — I was only sixteen, but I'll never forget the night we stood outside of Burger King. You told me that I will never be happy until I just be by myself. I have been holding onto that statement for a long time. Thank you.

To my fourth-grade teacher, Mrs. Haynes, and your assistant, Ms. Johnson — thank you for all your help; it will never be forgotten. Ms. Johnson was crazy about the color purple. I'd also like to thank Mrs. Jennings, the student counselor. Words cannot explain how much I appreciate all of you.

To my old boss who took me under his wing as if I were one of his own sons — you and your queen invested a lot in me. I did not listen most of the time (LOL), and unfortunately I sometimes learned the hard way. I love you both and wish you guys the best in your marriage.

Speaking of marriage, I would like to take this time to thank a woman I was once married to, Tracey Frazier. I took you through hell and back. Whether you'll ever believe me or not, my intentions were never to hurt you. Sadly, what I've done to you seems to haunt me from time to time. I cannot think of any individual who has put up with how I used to be more than you. You tried everything to show me you loved me. More than anything else, divorcing me was probably the best thing that you could have done for me, because it helped me start depending on God and to start crying out to him.

To my ex-mother-in-law, Mrs. Lisa — I want to thank you for all your help. Please forgive me for letting you down.

To Brittany Williams, my childhood friend — thank you for the help you gave my siblings and me. When we needed someone to talk to, you were there. Thank you for being obedient and letting God use you. Much love.

To Fyabird — with that word, you are a very humble brother. We have come a *long* way together. I have watched you go from being content, being single, to being married with a family. I love you, Fyabird, from the deepest pit of my soul.

Nadira Lewis (SAY NAH), I've watched you grow, too. I wish the best for you and your tribe.

904 Project Take Over, I love all of you. We have so many great memories of nights spent crying out to God, even those who used to associate with PTO. We all shared great times together.

To Pastor Craig Leverttee, a man that walks the walk — I have seen the tears you've cried while praying for people. No matter what people said or did to you, you still walked in love; you still kept a smile on your face. You were there for me through some of the roughest times of my life. No matter how I seemed to ignore what you told me, you hung in there with me. You, along with Ms. Andrews, spoke nothing but life over me. I will say that you denied yourself quite often for the sake of others. I thank you for preaching those hardcore messages; they saved my life.

To Felix Williams, my dirty, my round, my ace—I love you, bro. I hope that I will never forget about you. I believe in you, bro.

You both have a *powerful* testimony.

Mr. Earl, you poured a lot into me. You prayed for me; you mentored me. Thank you for your patience.

James Vancourt, thank you for looking out for me when I was down. You allowed me to crash at your spot several times, and you always fed me. I learned a lot from you. Much love, bro.

Uncle John and Alisha, the McGriff family, Brandon Thomas, Charles Baker ("Big Bruh"), Vari (been a long time coming from a mighty struggle), Benny, Uncle Supp Marquis, Deron and Imari Frazier, my siblings—I love you all.

This man needs a trophy or a plaque: Florida State College's very own Ed Jones. This man helped me get my high school diploma. Thank you for your patience and motivation.

T'Juan, you played a big role in my life. We shared some great moments together.

To my Auntie Michelle—you have gone the extra mile for me in so many ways. You have never, ever given up on me. You have always believed in me. I love you, Auntie.

E-Train, Lumare, Galen Workcuff, Corey Sanders—thank you.

I must thank a woman who helped me out tremendously. You gave me six words that I will hang on to *for the rest of my life*: "Live in reality and not falsehood." Her name is Jaundalyn Haywood, and I want to thank you, ma'am.

To my brother Preme Da Messenger—we on a mission for souls.

To Kevin and Mrs. Helin—I appreciate you guys for opening your home and refrigerator to me. Kevin, we have shared some father-and-son moments together.

Lastly, I want to thank one who has challenged me to grow; one who has not been my cheerleader, but encouraged me to grow in such a way that it hurt 80 percent of the time when we were together; someone who has been there for it all: my mentor/friend/big brother, Jerry Durr. (Why y'all looking at me?) No matter what wind may blow our way, no matter when the season comes that we'll have to part ways, I will always have a high level of respect for you. Keep it one hundred.

The thank-you train must come to a halt. So, to everyone who has made a difference in my life, whether good or bad, I want to say, all of you helped me grow into the man I am today. Thank you!

Introduction

When I first began to write this memoir at around the age of twenty one, someone told me that it wouldn't be read by anyone. So, I deleted what I had. I rewrote the first chapter months after and completed the first copy a few years later.

In my first copy, I did a lot of blaming others. I talked down to a lot of individuals. God has matured and stretched me quite a bit. I realized that there's no need to blame or talk down to anyone. I could have written this copy to the point that people would have been feeling so sorry for me. I do not need sympathy. I went through a lot in my childhood, but through it all, I am grateful. By the grace of God, look what I have become. It was unexpected, but the man does not have the final say.

A friend told me when I was about eighteen that it was going to be crazy how God was going to change my life. I must say, she was right. It's not easy being a "church boy." It has been hard. I have screamed and cried so much. I have had many lonely nights. There were so many times that I wanted to quit and do what I felt was easier. I have tried to quit, but I was surrounded by a few people who Abba sent my way who wouldn't let me quit. If it was not in God's plan, I would not be where I am today. My Heavenly Father saw the best in me when everyone else could only see the worst in me.

A sister asked me one day what I would change in my life. I told her, "Nothing." Every trial, every person, and all the pain have made me who I am today.

While I am still in the process of learning and growing, I stand by one of the most important principles in my life: "Embrace everything, including the pain, because it's all a part of the journey."

I AM . . .

I AM what my Creator made me.

> Although I go through hard times in my life, I will not let that faze me.

I AM not dumb.

I AM very smart.

I AM very different.

> I have been set apart.

I AM not a failure.

I AM mighty in all that I do.

> I will be different and stand strong.

> I will walk with my head up and stay true.

I AM not a quitter, but a giver, because of the leader that I AM.

> Even when I'm feeling stressed, maybe even a little depressed because things

> begin to look a mess,

> I will still be different because I KNOW WHO I AM.

> I will stay strong and be mighty and stand,

> showing the world who I really AM.

I Just Want to Be Remembered

Sometimes it's hard for me to go to sleep at night, because all that I think about is just how bad I want to succeed.

I don't wanna be like the next Martin Luther King, but God has given this boy here a dream.

I don't care about my name being remembered, but I do want to create a legacy that will hopefully live long after me, like the months in a year: August, September, October, November, December.

I just wanna create a legacy that will hopefully live long after me, like the seasons in a year: spring, fall, summa, and winta.

I said I . . . I just wanna be remembered for one who didn't settle for the title of a loosa, but a winna.

I just wanna be remembered as a trend-setta; not a begga, but a giva; not a borrower, but a lenda.

I wanna be remembered as one who laid down his life for the sake of othas, like for the sake of his brotha, fatha, or motha.

I just wanna be remembered.

You see, life is short, and I realize that.

And I realize that once I'm dead and gone, I'll never get this life back. I only got one shot, so while I'm here, I might as well give it all that I got until the tick-tock on my life clock stop.

I said I . . . I just wanna be remembered.

And I don't know when God is going to scream, "Timba!" and call my numba, but when he does, I hope that I am right with him so I don't have to go unda for eva and eva.

I said I . . . I just wanna be remembered.

When they mention my name, I don't want them to remember me with words such as "selfish," "greedy," or "gain." I don't even want to be associated with that word called "shame."

I don't want to be remembered as one who chased wealth, all for the purpose of himself, but he was help; he gave all that he was for everyone else.

I said I . . . I just wanna be remembered.

The other day, me and my pops had a deep phone conversation, and he asked me a question, and he said, "Son, what is your life's ultimate goal and motivation?" And with no hesitation I replied, "I . . . I just want to impact lives."

For I am just a farmer boy planting and watering seeds, hoping to give back life to all those people who have given up on all their hopes, their visions, and dreams.

And for all of you who have given up on all your hopes, your visions, and your dreams, I just want to encourage you to get back to dreaming. Get your light back, and get back to beaming.

For there is so much more in store for you, so let's all talk less and do more.

Like the months in a year—August, September, October, November, December—I said I . . . I just . . . I just want to be remembered.

This Woman

She challenges me to take our friendship slow. She has taught me how to not rush it, but to let what is meant to be flow.

'Cause before, I would try to rush into things like a hot shower. I be trying to find different ways to wow her, 'cause this woman here is worth more than a vase of colorful flowers. She's made me want to man up and stop being a coward.

Usually when a woman doesn't respond back after I hit 'em up, I be ready to cut them off, but not this one. When she doesn't pick up, I know that she's busy, and whether it's the same day or the next day, she always gets back with me. That's why for this woman, I don't mind waiting patiently. She's a beautiful masterpiece. She's got it going on, from her head, her waist, and her feet.

There's so much I wanna know about this woman. This woman is historical. Her smile doesn't even make sense to be called horrible, because her smile is adorable.

I don't hear from this woman much, but when I do, I be wanting to sing a song as though I got da blues.

We only hung out one time, so I don't understand how this woman is always on my mind as though she were a test that I wasn't ready for, like a test I knew I wasn't going to pass. Ask me my favorite comedian and I'll give you her name, 'cause she knows exactly what to say to make me laugh, and most of the time she don't even be joking. She just be keeping it real. I said she trill.

I'm doing good, but she makes me wanna do betta, and that's why for this woman, I didn't have to struggle to write this poem. I wouldn't even mind writing her a four-page letta, because this woman is worth all of my time and smiles. This woman is worth all the while.

This woman is you.

Where It All Began

It all started on October 7, 1989, in a hospital in Kennesaw, Georgia. At two a.m. early Saturday, a baby was born. His name was Derrick Leroyal Frazier Jr. Yes, folks, that's me. Out of all those billions of egg cells, God chose me; I did not choose to be born. God created me for a divine purpose. I was born into a family of four, until 1990, when my beautiful little sister, Imari, was born. Momma stopped having children after her. So, there we were: the Frazier family of five.

I have always loved my family, and despite the many turbulences that we faced on our individual journeys and our journey as a family, I see all of it as a lesson that has enabled me to be the humble, resilient individual that I strive to be today. The morals and values that I cherish today all have to do with the ones instilled at an early age when we were forced to go to church as a family. Then, I did not understand the importance, but now I do.

My parents took us to church all the time. We went to church Sunday morning, Sunday night, Wednesday night, Thursday night, and Saturday for choir rehearsal and to help clean up the church. My parents would have us read three chapters of the Bible every morning. If they felt like we read it too fast, they would tell us to go back and read it again. Honestly, reading three chapters of the Bible every morning was boring. I was always the one that had to go back and reread my chapters again.

In my household, my parents were very stern. There was no talking back; you did as you were told. It was either "yes sir" or "no sir," "yes ma'am" or "no ma'am." Talking back? Man, please! We were too scared to even try and explain ourselves to our parents. I think one time I tried to talk back to my mom. I was not being disrespectful, but apparently my dad thought so. My dad hit me upside my head so hard, I saw colored stars. The way that some of these kids today talk to their parents amazes me. They wouldn't have lasted half a day in our home.

When we would go out in public, we were always on point. My parents taught us how to pick out our clothes and iron them at a young age. My parents were our barber and hairstylist. I liked it better when Mom cut my hair because she would attempt designs, unlike when my dad did it. She would hook us up with a nice, clean cut. Dad seemed like all he knew was the good-old bald head.

We were not a rich family. We did not have a big house in the mountains. Even though we didn't have a big bank account or the most expensive material things, my parents made ends meet. My parents always kept a job, especially my dad. If my mom was not working, my dad always had a job. He was not a man that sat at home all day while his woman worked hard. He has always been a great example in terms of someone who was hardworking.

Growing Up

I think it's safe to say I was the black sheep among my siblings. I was always the one getting in trouble. I used to get in trouble for talking too much in class. I guess I was only practicing for what I would be doing for the rest of my life: inspirational speaking. When my report card came home, it would always say that I was not following directions. In our house, reports like this called for an automatic whooping. I got more bad reports than my brother and sister. There was this paper in school called a "midterm slip." It was a white, rectangular-shaped piece of paper that showed the parents how we were doing in school. I hated that paper. It seemed like all the teachers checked off all the bad things I was doing wrong. It was like the teachers wanted me to get a whooping.

School was more like a playground for me. I was always on punishment at home and getting whoopings, so I figured I may as well have a good time in school. I was always that kid that all my teachers wanted to have a parent conference with. I hated parent conferences. I remember my mom taking a belt to one conference, and she said if she heard anything bad that she was going to use it. She was serious. The teacher told my mom that I was cutting up. When we left the conference, my mom hit me with the belt right outside the classroom. It was early in the morning, so a lot of kids did not see me get hit.

As you can see, my parents did not believe in holding back on that rod. They believed in using it. I remember that my dad used to always tell us that every time we got out of line, we were going to get it. I am convinced that that had to be my dad's favorite lines: "Every time you get out of line . . . "

To be honest, I would not even call it a whooping. It felt like I was being beaten all the time, the way my dad would throw that arm back as if he were on a baseball team trying to hit a home run. My parents always told us that they whooped us because they loved us. That never made sense to me, especially not as a young boy. How is whooping love? And every time they did whoop me, it seemed like they were trying to beat the color off my skin.

Now that I am older, I can understand what my parents meant. Proverbs 22:15 says that "Foolishness is bound up in the heart of a child, but the rod of discipline will remove it far from him" (BSB). I do not agree with all of the methods that they used to discipline me—things like not feeding me and making me sleep on the floor instead of my bed when I was only eight years old. I feel like my parents went too far sometimes. It took me awhile to realize this, but when a parent is trying their best to provide for their family but also dealing with that one child that is always in trouble, it can make parents angry, which may cause them to do things that are out of frustration. However, children are children, and not every child is the same, and not every child learns the same. It may take a little more patience or love with the one who seems to be the black sheep.

Maybe my parents did attempt simple discipline. I guess the more trouble I got into, the worse it got. I do not remember receiving many hugs or kisses from my parents. I do not recall them telling me that they loved me or were proud of me. A child's lack of attention and love can negatively affect them when they get older. It can affect their future relationships with their friends or significant other. A child needs to know that they are loved and cared about, even the ones that seem like they are always getting into trouble.

I remember one day my parents took me to pass a prison, and told me that if I did not "tighten up" that the prison would be my home. It never became my home. I have only been to jail one time for about ten hours for driving on a suspended license. I hated that place. The officers in jail treat you just like animals and act like everyone is a criminal. The crazy thing about when I went to jail is that when we pulled into the garage of the jail and the officer took me in, the first thing this female officer said was "Congratulations." I couldn't believe it. That's when I knew I was in the wrong place.

Besides that one time, I have never been in trouble with the law. I do not know the exact year, but my uncle, my dad's little brother, committed suicide. About a year later my Papa, my dad's stepfather, died. After their deaths took place, it seemed like our family went downhill.

Split Apart 3

My household turned upside down, and I started to see and experience changes that have affected my life and later became a part of my testimony. I remember one day my sister and I were told to walk straight home from school. We did as we were told, but decided to make a pit stop at the front office of our apartment. We didn't cause any trouble; we just wanted some candy. So, the landlady gave us some. Then we went and sat on the steps and waited for our mom to come home.

When she finally arrived home, we went in and started on our homework. Then I heard Mom ask Imari, my sister, where we went after school. My sister told her that we walked home and sat on the steps. My mom replied that that was not what we did. She said that my dad went to the front office, and the landlady told him that she gave us some candy. The landlady remarked that we were well-behaved children. Since my sister lied to my mom, we had to get a whooping.

I recall sitting on the bed scared, naked, and trembling to wait for my turn as my sister was getting her whooping in Mom's room. My dad came into the room and said something to me, and then he went back to the room where my sister was getting punished. Until this day I don't know how, but I quickly put on a jacket, pants, and shirt and ran out the door. I didn't have on any socks or shoes. I was literally running for my life. If you've ever watched a deer or gazelle run from a lion, you know they are running for their lives. The gazelle has to outrun the lion because if it doesn't, it knows it will be caught and eaten. I was the gazelle that day. Grass burrs were sticking in my feet, but I kept running.

This was the beginning of my new norm. I had gotten to the point where I was tired of the pain of my parents beating on me. I hated it so bad. It was so bad that when my dad started beating me, I would cry out for help. I remember him asking me who was going to help me, and all I brought my young lips to say was "Jesus." When I said that name, he stopped. Calling on Jesus did something for me from a tender age.

I started to go to school and tell my teachers and guidance counselors what was going on with me at home. Eventually, the teachers started to get involved. One day after I ran away, when I went to school the teacher saw some bruises on me. That was the day that the Department of Children and Family Services took me and my siblings away from our parents. They moved us in with our grandma.

I was glad we moved. We changed schools, and now my life was different. There was only one incident where

I was scared to go home. I forget what exactly happened, but I knew I was in trouble. Grandma wasn't mean to us, but when it was needed, she'd put her foot down and give us a whooping when we deserved it. I think we only stayed with her for a year or two.

My siblings and I ended up going to family counseling with our parents. We would go to those meetings and say nothing. Even if we wanted to say something, we wouldn't because we were so scared of them. I don't think my brother or sister had a problem with my parents. They weren't bad, but they had their days when they got a good beating, too.

Slowly but surely, we began to work our way back home. We began by going back to my parents' house on the weekends. They were so nice and sweet to us. Even though I didn't want to live with them again, I was forced to go on those visits.

Because they were being so nice, it made me feel like I wanted to go back and live with them. During our weekend visits, they would let us stay up late and play the Nintendo. They gave us ice cream and we would have a good time. I really did feel the love. I don't know if they were just being nice because they had to or what. But, whatever the reasons, it was working.

Eventually, we moved back in with our parents. It wasn't long before things went back to the way they used to be. I kept running away from home because I didn't want to be there anymore. I was only eleven or twelve when I ran and met a friend. I had this friend I went to school with who introduced me to this lady who, coincidently, lived in our apartments. My friend told me that the lady would give us some candy and that I could spend the night at her house. The lady appeared to be in her early twenties, wasn't married, and stayed by herself. I would lie to her and tell her that my parents said it was all right for me to spend the night at her house. Some days she would just leave me in the house by myself and I would watch TV and eat the whole time.

Then, I discovered that she had pornographic tapes in her closet. When she would leave, I would get the tapes from her closet and watch them. I spent weekends at her house for a few weeks straight. Then one day as she was taking me home, I told her that I had been lying to her. She ended up taking me home and telling my parents what I was doing, but that didn't stop me from running away again.

Soon after that, I started stealing lunch money from my brother and sister. I wasn't eating enough at home, so I would steal their money and buy extra food at school. Even if I didn't steal their money, I would always beg for other kids' lunches at school. There was this guy in my class whose mom gave him a candy bar every day, and he always kept it in the front part of his backpack. He always left his backpack on the back of his chair, and every day I would steal his candy bar while he was sitting in his seat.

I got so good at stealing that my mom started searching me before I went to school. She would make me take all the stuff out of my book bag and check my pockets. She would search me from head to toe.

My dad started driving trucks and would come home later from work. There was one incident where my sister and I came home from school and I hit her. That was the worst thing I could have done. My dad hated when we fought. That was the day they decided to take me to the Youth Crisis Center, a place for troubled youth and runaways. They were trying to teach me a lesson. I ended up loving that place. I stayed at the Youth Crisis Center for about six months. I was around other young males such as myself who were also going through a crisis at home.

After spending those six months there, I went home and ran away a few more times. One of those times I even convinced my brother to run away with me. It was crazy. We ran to the Youth Crisis Center together. Eventually, we had to go back home, but I had decided that enough was enough for me. I made up my mind that the next time I ran away from home, I was not coming back.

Our family moved into this nice house on the west side of Jacksonville, Florida. When you opened the front door, there was a room with a couch and a radio. It was more like a quiet room. There was another door that opened into the living room, bathrooms, kitchen, and the den. You could lock this door and be separated from the rest of the house.

After my parents got tired of me running away and stealing money, they would lock me in the front room away from everybody and everything else. At night when I had to use the bathroom, I would use the restroom through a screen window in the laundry room, which was also in this little room. One day, my mom unlocked the door and set a bowl of cereal on the ground and told me that was my breakfast. It was early in the morning, about 6:00 a.m. After eating the cereal, my stomach started hurting. I had to have a bowel movement. I used the bathroom on the floor, got some rags, cleaned it up, threw it in a pillowcase, and ran away again. That was the last day I ever stayed with my parents again. I ran away and did not return.

One night while roaming the streets, I met this drug dealer in some apartments called Eureka Gardens. These apartments were known for their high rate of crime. As I was walking past this dude, he asked me if I wanted him to call me a taxi to take me home. I told him no. I didn't want to go home. I told him a little bit of my story, and he told me to take a ride with him. I didn't know this dude from Adam or Eve, but I still got in the car with him.

He drove me to some other apartments on a street called Shirley Avenue, not far from Eureka Gardens. We went into one of the apartments and I saw this guy with one leg in a wheelchair. Red, the drug dealer, took the guy to the back and talked with him. When they came out of the room, they told me I would be staying there.

In the living room was a nice bed on the floor. The bed was sitting on a two-by-four that looked like a box spring. It was cool for me, and there was even a TV in the front room. The dude treated me like a son. He fed me, gave me a few dollars, and was even trying to get me back into school. They brought me shoes and clothes, and took care of me.

One day after I had gone to work with the apartment manager, I came back to the house and there were private police cars in the parking lot. I recognized that one of the cars belonged to my friend's dad who was a policeman. Come to find out, the man I was staying with had gotten robbed in broad daylight. The guy always left his front door open, and people knew he was selling drugs.

After that, we moved down the street to some other apartments. By this time, the guy had me call my dad and talk to him about putting me in school. My dad approved, and he got me in school. I guess by this time my dad was fed up with me and felt like whatever I was doing was fine.

I ended up going to Lake Shore Middle School. I wasn't at the school for more than a month. I fell out with the guy and we went our separate ways. I ended up going back to Shirley Avenue and staying with the apartment manager. The police were always picking me up and dropping me back off at the Youth Crisis Center. I would stay the night, eat, and run away the next day.

One night I ran away and came back to the apartments. As I was walking up, somebody told me that I had just missed the shootout. Red and another drug dealer had gotten into a fight. Red was on top of the other guy beating him up and got shot a couple of times. The other guy had moved into the apartments and was selling drugs. However, the apartments were Red's spot, and he had it on lock. They told me Red hopped over a wall, collapsed on the next street, and called 911. Basically, Red fought him because he felt that his territory was invaded, which meant less money for Red.

God was protecting me out there in those streets. Anything could have happened to me. I could have been raped, hit by a car, or beaten to death. I could have been shot. One night the police kicked in the door where I was staying. The police were looking for drugs. I don't know how that story ended, because I wasn't there at the time. If I had been there, I could have gotten in major trouble. I didn't cause any trouble in the street, but just being associated with the wrong people made me look bad.

There were so many street fights that I could have been involved in, but I didn't get into any fights because I would always run. I was horrified by somebody beating on me. So, my feet became my way to escape from everything. All I knew how to do was run from pain.

Running from things became a lifelong thing. I never regretted running away from my parents' house. To me, I feel like that was the right thing to do. It helped me out a lot. However, there were some moments when I shouldn't have run. Maybe there's someone reading this book that may be running from something, just like that gazelle running from the lion. I would like to encourage you by saying *yes*, there are some things that you should run from, and there are things that you have to learn to man up and face. You should not run from your responsibilities, your calling, and the Heavenly Father. I've tried to run from Him, too. Running from God is very foolish, because He sees and knows our every move.

I want to challenge you today, too. Be real with yourself. Is there anything that you are running from? If there is, I challenge you to face it. Life is going to be hard sometimes, but I learned that pain equals growth. Pain is a part of life. Life will never be easy. I once heard someone say that it's not about how hard you can hit, but how hard of a hit you can take.

As I close out this part of my life, I want to say this: my pastor told me that someone helped him look at his trials differently. He said our trials are like a tunnel. At the end of the tunnel, there is a light.

Foster Care

One day I was chilling in the apartments on Shirley Avenue. Somehow the Department of Children and Family Services found out where I was staying. They came to pick me up, but at the time I was in somebody else's house. They came back the next day and got me. The caseworker took me back to her office, and after doing all the paperwork, she took me to my first foster home.

I don't have much to say about my first foster mother. All I remember about her was that she didn't play any games and she had a lot of rules. There were nights when I would get dropped off at the house and I would have to stand outside until my foster mother decided to come home.

She enrolled me in this school called Northwestern Middle School. I had never heard of that school before. I would get on the school bus and sit right in the front. I didn't have any family or friends at all at that school, so I made sure I sat close to the bus driver and the door.

On the second day of school, there was this kid who started talking about me. His friends started laughing and asking me if I was going to let him talk about me. Being a kid, of course, I said something back to him. Whatever my exact words were, he didn't like it. When we got on the bus that afternoon, he let it be known to me and everyone else that he wanted to fight me the next day. Some people told him not to fight me and others told him to do it. On the other hand, I wasn't having that at all.

The next day I woke up and got dressed like it was a normal school day. I walked slowly to the bus stop and watched the bus pass by. Yes, I missed the bus. Do you really think I was going to get on that bus? No sir! Those kids could have jumped me. I was the new, unknown kid on the block.

I never went back to that school. I got on the JTA bus and went back to Shirley Avenue. Later on that day, my caseworker from DCF found me at the apartments. She picked me up and took me back to her office. This time I was going to another foster home.

My caseworker introduced me to a lady named Joyce Andrews. I must have sat in her office for hours. Eventually, we left and went to her house. I walked into her house and was blown away. It was beautiful. Her house looks twenty times better now than it did when I grew up in it. She introduced me to her friend Mr. McGee. They laid down the rules and talked with me about how they did things.

It was, like, seven of us living in the house, including her birth son. The majority of the guys didn't want me there. After being there for a while, I understood why. Ms.

Andrews, or "Auntie," as I called her, had us spoiled. We were living a life that 99.9 percent of foster-care kids don't get to experience. Auntie gave us the world.

On Saturday, we cleaned the house from top to bottom, and I do mean from top to bottom. We had to clean our rooms, the living room, ceiling fans, china cabinets, and the garage. This wasn't a small house, this was a nice-sized house with tons of things in it. She stayed on our backs until that house was spotless. After we got done with our chores, she would give us a few dollars.

Ms. Andrews taught us how to catch the bus, get a haircut, go to the movies, and be back home on time. She taught us how to be young men and not to depend on anyone. I didn't really learn that lesson until I turned twenty-three. To be honest, I'm still learning that lesson.

There were some heated moments, and we did a lot of clowning on each other. There were days when my foster mom's son just wanted to be alone with her. Come to think about it, I would be that way, too, if my mom kept all these boys and was paying them a lot of attention. I didn't understand a lot of things when I was younger. Now that I'm older and much wiser, I understand a lot more.

In the foster-care system, I never knew who my friends were. I would see kids come and go. I would be sharing a room with someone one week, and the next week they'd be gone. There were a few guys who wound up going back to their natural families. That wasn't the case with me.

There was one night when I was on the phone with my high school love and I began to think about my mom and dad. I started crying, because I really did miss them. Those were my parents, and being away from them was difficult. I loved them, I just didn't like the way they treated me.

I have been to a total of four foster homes. My worst experience was at this home on Phoenix Avenue. I think that's the northeast side of Jacksonville. After staying with Ms. Andrews for about six months, she needed to teach me a lesson. The lesson was "Don't think you're just going to be in my house and not say anything to me." LOL. I'll admit that I was disrespectful back then.

I'll never forget the day DCF picked me up from the high school I attended. They told me they were taking me for a ride. Then, it dawned on me that they were taking me to another foster home. When Ms. Andrews put someone out, they would never see it coming. She was always so calm and smooth about it. She would threaten us, but she said it so much that we never believed her. However, she knew exactly what she was doing. This particular day, she caught me slipping.

As we pulled up to my new foster home, I saw there were flies everywhere. The house was also much smaller than what I was used to. The next morning, my new foster mom cooked us breakfast. She had it smelling good. She cooked sausage, eggs, and pancakes. She put everything on one plate and handed it to me. I'm thinking, *It's my food.*

Then, she tells me to split up the food with the other guys. *What?* It was, like, five of us. I'm not even joking. We drank out of nasty Styrofoam cups. It was horrible. All we did at this home was smoke weed, smoke weed, and smoke more weed. We fought even if we didn't want to fight, because the other foster boys made us fight. We fought in and outside the house.

One morning, my foster mom called the police on us because we didn't go to school. The police officer picked all of us up and took us to some little center. It wasn't a detention center, just a place where they held kids who didn't go to school that day. We didn't like going to school because we barely had clothes to wear. I only had two or three outfits. The clothes that I had were either lost or stolen. It was ridiculous.

I begged Ms. Andrews to let me come back. It was torture.

I stayed there for about two months, and then I got moved to another home. The next home was cool. The foster mom was more like a grandma. It was just me and another little boy who stayed with her. She always took us to church. When I was staying with her, I barely went to school, and she never forced me to. During that time, I was a student at Andrew Jackson High School. I was going through so many changes, I didn't care about learning anything. During the day, I just stayed on the chat line until I met someone.

Eventually, Ms. Andrews let me come back. I had learned my lesson.

Foster care was like an adventure; it was always different—different counselors, some of whom I liked, some of whom I didn't. A lot of caseworkers, as well as some of the foster parents, were and still are only in it for the money. There are very few who really have a heart for the children. I'll never forget about this one caseworker I had. At first, I thought she was cool, then people started telling me how caseworkers weren't so cool. So, I and my used-to-be big mouth would go back and tell my caseworker how I couldn't stand her. I would leave her voicemails saying that I knew she didn't care about me. I treated her bad, even though she wasn't. I was just listening to what others were saying. Somehow, I realized that I was wrong and I apologized to her. She told me that she was just about to give my case to someone else.

How Foster Care Changed My Life

Anyone who knows me should know that I try to keep it as real as possible. When people are real, people connect better.

My weakness in life has always been women. I started watching porn videos around the age of eleven or twelve. I would have these images of me having sex with girls in my elementary school. One night before I got into foster care, I had run away from home. I had a male friend who let me sleep in his backyard on this lawn chair. In his family shed, his dad kept a bunch of magazines full of naked women. I spent hours upon hours just looking at those magazines.

Then, I went from the magazines to VHS tapes. This was way before anyone knew about DVDs. Once I got into foster care, I lost my virginity. I had girlfriends in elementary school, but I never had intercourse with them.

When I was running the streets, I would lust for some of those girls, but I never lost my virginity. It never went past a certain point. One day, another foster brother and I started talking about sex. He told me that once I started having sex that I would want more. I wanted that to happen, but I didn't believe what he was saying. (By the way, I'm not saying this to encourage anybody to go and have sex. If you are having sex outside of marriage, it's wrong. It will always be wrong until you get married.)

Sure enough, he was right. I started dating this young lady who was in foster care, but in a different home. She and my sister were staying in the same foster home, so that's how we met. She had way more sexual experience than I did. One night, I and a few other people went to a park up the street. I was sixteen years old, and on that night, I let her take my virginity.

Being a virgin doesn't seem cool, but in reality, the one that you marry is the one who you should have that experience with. That goes for a man or a woman. If you give up your virginity to the one that is not your husband or wife, you're robbing your future spouse of what's theirs.

It's crazy these days how they advertise sex everywhere. It's on the billboards, TV, and the worst place, the internet. The whole internet is rotten. They even advertise sex in video games. The cartoons are even worse.

I feel for kids these days. I know it's hard. I was addicted to pornography. I was into sex, phone sex, and masturbation. I was into it all. I enjoyed it while I was doing it, but afterward, I always felt drained. I would tell God I was sorry and be right back at it seconds later.

Drugs and Alcohol

I was already drinking and smoking weed before I got into foster care. I was exposed to drugs at about age fourteen. I was also smoking weed mixed with cocaine at the same age.

Foster care exposed me to a lot. I met a lot of people and I have seen a lot of things, both good and bad. Through all of my years of running away and being in foster care, I continued to pray.

In my teenage years, I desired to be somebody that people knew. I wanted to fit in and feel like I was a part of something, whether it was good or bad. I dealt with a lot of low self-esteem growing up. I used to think that I was the ugliest dude ever. Even though I always had a girlfriend, I would still feel ugly.

I used to think that all my foster brothers were better than me. There were days when we would go to the mall or the movies and they would dress so nice. In my eyes they had swag, they had money saved, and they had all the girls. They were doing well in school. I mean, they had it going on.

I would try so hard to get some of the guys in foster care to like me. It was one guy who used to ask me to do everything for him. If he asked me to wash his shoes, I would do it. If he asked me to get the remote, I did. Whatever he wanted, I would do it. I was like his "do" boy. I only did it to be accepted. When someone really wants to fit in, they'll do just about whatever it takes.

I would write letters and tell God what I desired. Sure enough, he answered my prayers. There is a saying that goes "God may not come when you want him, but he's always on time." I know I talk about God a lot, but I cannot help it. This is my testimony about how I came through my tunnel. If God brought me through, He can do the same for you.

I got my first job at sixteen. I worked at Burger King. It was a nice experience. It wasn't easy at first. It took me forever just to learn how to put ketchup, mustard, and pickles on a burger. I learn very differently from most people. When people are explaining things to me, it's like they literally have to tell me one hundred times before I get it. That's just how I learn.

While working at Burger King, I was still a high school student. My routine was to stay on the phone all night. Some nights I would stay on the phone until five o'clock in the morning. I would take a quick nap, wake up, get dressed, walk to the bus. and go to school. When I got to school, I would sleep in most of my classes, and I would often get tardy slips for being late to class. I stayed in in-school suspension (ISSP). I was in the ESE classes. I wasn't stupid, I just didn't want to be in the regular classes and do all the hard work. Not only would I go to sleep in my classes, but I would curse out my teachers.

The funny thing is that it wasn't hurting them, it was only hurting me. They had their diplomas and degrees. There was one thing I found interesting in high school. It was the fact that the kids who were laughing with me were passing me by. It seemed like we were all clowning around. Somehow, at the end of the school year, they were going to the next grade. On the other hand, I was failing and repeating the same grade again.

I repeated ninth grade twice. I didn't even make it to the tenth grade. Eventually, the principal kicked me out of high school. One reason was because I received too many referrals. I got written up for skipping class, breaking the school bus window, sexual harassment, and being disruptive in class. I was reckless. Even though I had poor behavior and was uncool in high school, I did have a chance to experience a moment that I never thought I would. That moment was prom.

It was my high school sweetheart's eleventh-grade prom, and she was taking me, of course. The whole experience of going to pick out my suit and getting prepared was beautiful. I had never experienced anything like it. I was dressed in a white suit with the hat, gloves, and the cane. I didn't take the cane to prom (LOL). I was cleaner than a pair of all-white Air Force Ones. My date was stunning. I had never seen her look more gorgeous, and together we shined like the moon on a cloudless night. I didn't even know how to dance, so she found other dance partners, which hurt a bit. Nevertheless, I sat back and watched her enjoy herself. She had one more year left in school. Overall, it was good.

Experiences like those are priceless. I had also had the chance to be in the Navy Junior Reserve Officers' Training Corps (NJROTC) program and play in the band. My instrument of choice was the tuba. I didn't know how to read music. The songs I knew how to play were learned by watching someone else.

Once, at band rehearsal, I was the only tuba player there. Everybody else was in their instrument group while I stood alone. We started going over songs, but on one of the songs the tuba players had to start it off. Since I was the only tuba there, I had to start it off, but I didn't know how to. Everybody turned around and looked at me. It was so embarrassing. You know you're embarrassed when you start sweating under your armpits! The drummer boys ended up doing my part.

I've always been the oddball, no matter where I go. When I went to parties, I would always have to get twice as drunk as other people just to have a good time. I couldn't be sober and have a good time. I would always feel out of place if I wasn't intoxicated. I guess that was a sign that that wasn't the life for me.

My foster mom always said that I was a praying boy. She would always call me a preacher. Back then, I didn't believe her. She would tell me that I was going to make it. Sometimes it's hard to believe something you can't see. I sort of believed her, but it just seemed too good to be true.

Most of my foster brothers are doing pretty good for themselves. Some made the wrong choices and now they're incarcerated. Only one of them died. He was only seventeen or eighteen. One day he was smoking weed that someone had laced with something bad. He went to sleep, and his heart burst in his sleep. What's sad is, it should have been me.

There are a few brothers that are still trying to find their way. Then there are the few who have learned how to make it in life. Those few are doing excellent for themselves. One has already received two degrees from college. He is currently a counselor for other foster kids.

I love my foster brothers and I'm very proud of them. They know that I would give them the shirt off my back if they needed it. I can't judge the ones that are incarcerated or the ones who settled for an average life. For the ones who are still trying to find their way, I can only love them and keep them lifted up. My hope for all of my foster brothers is that they never give up on life, no matter how hard it may seem. Giving up on life is the worst thing any human being could ever do.

We owe it to ourselves to be the *best men* that we can be. I wish the best for all foster-care kids. It's not an easy thing, especially for the ones who don't have anyone in their corner. The best thing that I could tell any foster child is to make up your mind that you will make it in life. More than that, pray. Pray that God will lead you to do the right thing. Pray that He will send the people your way that will help you.

You have a purpose for being here. Everything that you are going through is for a reason. Your birth was not a mistake. Out of all those billions of eggs in your parent's sperm, you were chosen for a reason.

So, don't give up. There are people who are depending on you to make it. In the words of a motivational speaker I once heard, "Don't cry to quit, cry to keep going."

The Turnaround

At the age of eighteen, I was still staying with my foster mom, as long as I paid her. It wasn't long until I had to move. Right before I moved out, I ran into some guys called the "Duval Pretty Boys." They were known for their dances and their music. Most of the young girls were crazy in love with them.

One night they popped up at my foster mom's house and we talked about a few things. We discussed my interest in getting involved with the band, and about a week later I joined the group. I was trying to find myself, so I thought the group would be a good fit. It was some experience. The best part, for me, was getting into the clubs for free and getting more attention from girls.

One day we agreed to meet at their house, as they wanted to show me this new dance they created. The dance was to be performed to a song called "Crank that Church Boy." It was written by a local artist named T'Juan. They started telling me how they were getting ready to go out of town with this dude. I was excited, jealous, and feeling left out at the same time. They tried to teach me the dance, but I didn't catch on quick enough.

I ended up meeting T'Juan the next day. He was very different from the Pretty Boys. He was a positive guy. I tried hard to impress him. Again, I just wanted to be accepted. After I met T'Juan, he introduced me to Mr. and Mrs. Estell. I guess you can say they were his godparents. I know for sure Mrs. Estell was his pastor. They were some of the nicest people that I had ever met. They fed us and made us feel like family.

The Pretty Boys and I took a road trip with T'Juan. The whole ride to Atlanta, the leader of the Pretty Boys talked about me. He talked about my clothes and everything that was wrong with me. He made me feel as low as the ground. On the trip, I met another guy named Brandon who heard the guys picking on me. He told me not to worry about it.

When we finally got back to Jacksonville, it was late at night. As I was getting my belongings, I noticed that my Bible was missing. It turned out that one of the guys had hit somebody with it and lost it on the van. This specific Bible was very special to me. From that night on, I told myself I was done with the whole Pretty Boy thing.

The following day was Sunday. That night I went with T'Juan to the Estells' church. Mrs. Estell spoke over my life like no one had done since I was young. After that church service, I went home and threw all my Pretty Boy chains and star earrings away. I was done.

The year was 2008, the year of new beginnings. It was a new season for all of us. Brandon and T'Juan had become the brothers I never had. Brandon was and still is a very good dancer. This brother is a dancing machine. He took the time to show me how to do the Church Boy dance. T'Juan and the Estells dismissed the Pretty Boys, and I was promoted as one of the main dancers.

So, there it was: T'Juan, the Estells, their daughter, Brandon, and me. We did everything together. We traveled, cranked it up, slept, cried, ate, and argued together. We had become a family.

I used to ask God to take me around the world. I asked Him to take me to places that I never thought I would go. God answered my prayers. I haven't been around the whole world yet, but I have traveled. I've been to St. Louis, South Carolina, Atlanta, and so many other places. I have been to gospel award shows, such as the Stellar Awards. I have met and shaken hands with several secular and gospel artists. I've met artists that people idolize and pay hundreds of dollars to see.

About a year later, T'Juan and some of us that were traveling with him started bumping heads. I guess for me, I wanted more attention. There was a lot of gossiping and betrayal going on within our circle and from others who were on the outside. The one thing I'd learn is that what one hangs around long enough is what one will eventually become. The more successful T'Juan became, the more successful I became.

I'd always been a writer, but around this time I started writing poetry. I started writing for this lady I met that stayed in the same apartment complex as me. One of my foster brothers who stayed next door to her introduced us. He told me to talk to her because she was a good, spiritual woman. She was older than me, but very smart and mature. We were not dating, but we were friends who found each other attractive. She loved my poems and constantly encouraged me to keep writing. She even advised me to start performing my poems at this place called the Ritz Theater.

I continued to write. Eventually taking her advice, I decided to go to the theater and perform. I was very nervous, but I got on the mic and let it rip. The people loved it. Month after month, I went back to the poetry spot to perform my poetry. The nickname that the Pretty Boys had given me was "Pretty Boy D." When I started to hang around T'Juan, we changed it to "Church Boy D." Church Boy D was my stage name, which I have since outgrown. I am way more mature and much wiser now than I was back then. I have asked people politely to not address me by that name, but people do it anyway. Some people don't even know my real name. All they know is Church Boy. I can't even lie, it does feel good to hear someone call me Church or Church Boy every now and then, but I would rather just be called D or Derrick.

I kept writing poems, but there was one poem that became my hit single. The poem's title: "Who Is Me?" That one poem opened up a lot of doors for me. I started performing at poetry venues, churches, and even schools.

By that time, the relationship between T'Juan and I started to fade away. It ended after an incident occurred between him and another close friend of mine. I should have been a better brother and told him what happened. I was scared to tell him for the sake of another friendship. After that, we stopped talking. But since then, we have reunited. Not as much as we used to, but I'm always hearing he's doing well. No matter the good or bad, I love T'Juan and Brandon Thomas. They are family, and they have played a big role in my life.

My friends and foster brothers were all over my house playing this video game. At that time in my life, I was hanging around a drug dealer. He had cars, money, and women. He had a lot of the material things that I wanted. I told him that I wanted to sell drugs. Selling drugs and making money looked easy. I thought it was easy, but looks can be deceiving.

Another lesson I learned was to be your own man. We as people sometimes want to be like someone else. However, we don't even know the pain or what it took for that person to get to where they are. Be yourself. There's too many copycats in the world and not enough originals.

I started hanging around this guy more and more. Eventually, he saw that I was loyal and put me on selling drugs. I was selling crack. I only sold crack twice. I was used to chilling in the house with different girls all the time. He told me one day that I could not be booed up and that I needed to be in the streets making money. I realized at that moment that selling drugs wasn't for me. I called him over to the crib and told him that I couldn't do it anymore. He was not upset, but I could tell that he was a little disappointed.

It could have been worse. I knew what he was capable of doing to someone.

The Hookup

On October 7, 2009, I walked into Belk's clothing store. I was with one of my foster brothers and Auntie, my foster mom. Auntie was doing some shopping, like she always did. As we were leaving, I saw this girl who caught my eye in a brown outfit and black flats. I only saw her from the back at first, and then I saw her face. At that moment all I could think to myself was, *That is my kind of girl.* There was something so different about her that I could not resist.

I approached this young lady and learned her name was Tracey. I had to give her a brief summary of my life just to get seven numbers. For some reason, she was not trying to hear any game from me, at least not at first. After all of my hard work, she gave me her number. If I'm not mistaken, the next day we started hanging out. I had just moved out of my foster mom's house into a studio apartment on the north side of Jacksonville.

Tracey and I didn't start off being friends. We jumped straight into a relationship. After about a week, she wanted me to come to her house and meet her family. How could I ever forget that day? She was sweet as can be that night. I asked her to fix me something to eat before I came over. She fixed me some store-bought lasagna. She ended up burning the lasagna. But, as time went on, she began cooking like a pro.

About a month later, I moved in with Tracey and her family. I was behind on some tickets that I owed. By me moving in with Tracey, I was able to pay off some of the tickets. I was supposed to be saving, but we were always shopping.

When two people move in together, it's called "shacking up." Sex is for a marriage. Sex outside of a marriage is fornication. We were definitely fornicating a lot. It was not long until we had problems. I was still messing around with other women. Tracey got pregnant and had a miscarriage. She was stressed out a lot, and that's why she lost the baby.

I would go out of town and mess with other women. I was still smoking, drinking, watching porn, and going to church at the same time. I was living a double lifestyle. We would go to church, go home, and fornicate as if nothing was ever said. There are so many people who do the same thing. "What's done in the dark will all come into the light one day" had to be my mom's favorite saying.

I was never the type of guy that was faithful. I never settled down with one woman and felt completely satisfied. It's sad, because I have had some of the best women in the world. I'm not talking about dime pieces, but women who really loved me and did their best to show me that they loved me.

It was like any female that showed me attention, I fell for them. I loved attention and compliments. I would do just about anything for a woman to like me or show me more attention. I liked my old girlfriends, but I didn't know how to love them.

Although it started to be messy between Tracey and me, there were some good times. She started buying me clothes. She would pick me up and drop me off when I needed her to, etc. After a while, she started to let me drive her car, pick her up, and drop her off at work. Then, we started to go to church together. My pastor at that time said he saw some good things changing in me. I can say Tracey had a lot to do with that. Tracey did things for me that no one had ever done for me. She lavished me with this love I had never experienced before. I would even say she spoiled me.

We eventually moved out of her mom's house and got our own place. We were still doing things the wrong way. We were deceiving ourselves. Needless to say, we paid for our disobedience. Galatians 6:7 tells us clearly "Do not be deceived. God is not mocked, for whatsoever a man sows, that shall he also reap" (NHEB). Another scripture, James 1:15, states "Then when lust hath conceived, it bringeth forth sin; and sin, when it finished, it bringeth forth death" (KJV). If I don't know anything else, I know these scriptures live, and they mean exactly what they say.

Even though we were going to church and Bible study, things were still just wrong between us. I mean, we were both changing in a good way, but our relationship was still rocky. Things continued to get worse. One night she caught me on the phone texting someone. After that, she went into the living room and called one of her guy friends. I took her phone and broke it. It was not the last phone of hers that I broke. I broke at least five more. It seemed like every time she got a new phone, she would make me mad and I would break it.

There was one night we were laying down in the dark and I wanted to fornicate with her so bad. She would not let me because it was wrong. God was dealing with her on certain things. I, on the other hand, did not appreciate that she was telling me no. I got up and walked into the living room. When I came back into the room, I punched a big hole in the wall. I never felt as strong and angry as I did that night.

After that night, it seemed like every time I got mad, I would punch a hole in the wall. I had terrible anger issues back then. I'm not proud of this, I'm just being honest. This is probably the reality of most people's relationships right now. I treated her bad. I would beat on her and push her down.

One night, we were outside and I slammed her car door. I went into the house and she came in after me. On that day I found out to not underestimate the quiet woman. I'll admit that she made it very clear to me that night that she wasn't going to let me beat on her again. She let me have it. She was punching me in the face and scratching me. It was like she was fighting somebody in the streets. All I could do was put my hands up and plead with her to stop. I had a bloody lip afterward.

That wasn't the last night we fought. I was just more cautious of what I said when we got into arguments. I wasn't so quick to hit her, because I knew what she was capable of doing to me. This was one of the consequences for living in sin.

Ladies and gentlemen, boys and girls, please don't play around with sin. *Please*, it will kill you. To all my brothers, if you are hitting or verbally abusing your woman, stop it. I don't care how mad she makes you. She is the weaker vessel. Treasure her as your queen, not a punching bag.

Also, parents, if you're fighting in front of your children, shame on you. Be more considerate. Fighting in front of children can affect them when they get into relationships. Take it from someone who has experienced it. Kids watch everything, and they will remember a lot of things when they get older. Train your children the right way, and when they get older, they will not flee from it.

Tracey and I looked good together. Everywhere we went, we were color coordinated. I really didn't know how to dress up before she came into my life. She changed my wardrobe. Tracey had me looking GQ and I had her looking fabulous. She liked wearing exotic heels and outfits that stood out, and that's what I loved to see her in. Sometimes we would try and outdo each other. There were some days where we were jealous of what the other one had on! LOL. I loved those moments. We looked good on the outside, but on the inside, we were messed up. We had no peace, no joy, no nothing.

After a few months of us living together, I put her out. She would come to spend the night as if she were still living with me. One night, we came home from Bible study and she said something slick, like I was acting fake. I said something slick back, but I was trying to keep my cool. We had just gotten home from Bible study. Before I knew it, she spat on me, and that's when the bell went *Ding! Ding! Ding!*

We started fighting. We went from the bedroom to the closet and ended up in the living room. I take the blame for a lot of things that went wrong in our relationship, but don't get it twisted. Tracey had her moments when she showed out for no reason. She had some serious baggage, too. It was sad. I really believe that the fornication is what messed us up. Our relationship was crazy, but we didn't stop there.

Marriage

Reflecting on this part of my life is always the most difficult. I didn't value this woman while she was in my life. Sometimes it takes time for good things to come around. When good things do come around, if you are not prepared or ready, you'll lose out, and you may never get that chance again. So, treasure the people in your life, including those things that have been given to you. I really hope that someone will embrace this chapter and learn from it.

Tracey and I had started talking about getting married. We were planning a beautiful wedding on the beach. Little did we know, we would be getting married sooner than we expected.

There was a season where it seemed like everybody around us was getting married. One night, we went to our usual Bible study. During testimony time, we found out that there was this couple who was getting married. They hadn't been dating long, but they both were previously married before, so they had experience. Now, you know when Tracey heard that news she gave me that look like, "You need to tighten up." I could feel the pressure just by the look she gave me. I knew I wanted to be with her, I just wasn't ready for that kind of commitment. I told her many times before that I was going to marry her, but I just never got around to asking her.

We decided to get married on May 23, 2011. She told me that if I did not marry her that she was going to leave me, and I didn't want that to happen. So, I went along with it. It felt like it was a joke. It did not feel real to me, and I didn't have any happy feelings about getting married. I knew in my heart it was too early. In fact, I kept hearing, "Wait a few more months." It was loud and clear.

Being that I was afraid of her leaving me, I went with the flow instead of what was truly in my heart. Listening to our emotions and feelings sometimes can get us in trouble. Another reason I wanted to get married was so that we would not be fornicating anymore. I went ahead and married her at the courthouse. I was the only one dressed in a button-up shirt, tie, dress pants, and a blazer. On the other hand, she had on a regular shirt, jeans, and some slides. She was smiling, and I felt empty. I wanted to cry because I was not ready.

After we got married, we went home. I was quiet the whole ride home. I didn't want to show her that I wasn't happy about getting married, because she would have started crying and going off on me. I was asking myself, *What in the world did I just do?* We didn't tell our parents, nor did we talk it over with our pastor at the time, Pastor Craig.

When we finally began telling people, they were hurt. They wanted to participate in the ceremony. Tracey's mom cried. Who gets married without first telling their parents so they can be there? We as people can be so selfish sometimes. We were so immature. We didn't think anybody would be hurt. Our pastor was hurt; he wanted to talk it over with us before we made that move. A lot of folks were surprised, shocked, and disappointed. There were some other newlyweds that were happy for us.

Marriage is not supposed to be rushed. Get to know the person that you are talking about spending the rest of your life with. Make sure that you can be great friends with this person. Make sure that you all are on the same accord spiritually before anything else. I did not realize that when you get married, you are around each other all the time. You have to live with this person. You eat and sleep with, and see this person every day. When two people get married, they become one. It is no more "I" or "me." Those words go out the window the day you say, "I do."

Marriage goes way beyond sex. Sex is a great and wonderful, wonderful, wonderful benefit for two married people, but it's bigger than that. Many people get married and don't have a clue of what they're doing. That is why they divorce faster than they get married.

You also have to understand the role of a husband and wife, and the direction that the marriage is going to go. It is easy to get into a marriage, but it takes longer to get out of it. It cost one hundred dollars for a simple ceremony at the courthouse. It takes almost five hundred dollars to get a divorce.

Self-denial, sacrifice, sharing, compromising, working together, love, compliments, encouragement, and understanding one another are the ingredients of a good marriage. In a marriage, you have to learn your spouse's love language. Everyone has a love language. Over all these things, the main ingredient has to be God. A marriage without God is like a car without tires or rims; it will not go anywhere. I am speaking from experience, not from something I Googled.

The marriage between Tracey and I cost us a lot. We were on the road toward killing one another. There were times when we were both driving and we almost swerved off the road. I had done so much damage to her emotions and self-esteem that she started losing her mind.

One night, she dropped me off at a friend's house for a few nights. As I was walking away from the car, she pepper-sprayed me in the face. The spray was all in my mouth. I could hardly see or breathe.

She threw all my clothes away. I had nice clothes and nice shoes. She bagged it all up and got rid of it. When she threw my clothes away, that really hurt me. Most of the clothes I had around that time, people had just given them to me.

There were several times when she tried to run me over in daylight. She got on my Facebook page and said all types of stuff about me. It was crazy. It seemed like the more I tried to be a good husband, the more I was told I was not. The more right I tried to do, evil seemed to keep following me.

In late 2012, about the middle of November, things got hard in my personal life. I started to get these urges to drink and go to the strip clubs like never before. It got so bad that at work I could taste liquor on my tongue. I would drive to the strip clubs, sit for a while, and then leave because I knew it was wrong. My conviction would not let me go in. I was working in an atmosphere where just about everyone at my job was talking about clubbing and drinking. Almost everybody on my job was tatted up and had foul mouths. There were women on my job that wanted me, but initially, I didn't think too much of it. I was married, so I couldn't do anything with them. When I look back, I now understand that those women were being used by the enemy.

To be honest, if I was not married at that time, those ladies probably would not have been thinking about me. I was trying so hard to be faithful to Tracey, I really was. I even started to tell people I was married. For me, that was a humongous accomplishment, because I did not like people knowing that I was in a relationship, especially other women.

Within the same season, it seemed as though a lot of people I knew personally who were saints started to slip back to their old ways. I started to watch them fall. I did not like what I saw. I mean, there was some foul stuff going on. Instead of praying for them, I started to go wrong with them. I gave into the things that kept pulling at me. I started drinking and smoking. I even went to work and started to talk to one of the girls that wanted me. We started to hook up after work.

I just could not ignore what I was feeling any longer. I would leave home and be gone two to three nights at a time while Tracey was at home by herself. The really sad thing was that she still was trying her hardest to be a good wife. I have to give her credit.

I remember one night when I came home from a strip club, I was drunk and smelled like sex. I didn't have sex with a woman, but it was the smell of a woman who had been dancing on me. I'll never forget that night. I opened our bedroom door and walked to the edge of the bed, and Tracey reached out her arms to me. The way she reached out her arms to me was like how a mom does to her baby that just needs a hug. That's another reason why I couldn't get enough of her. She was my wife, but she showed me this motherly love that I never felt. She always knew how to connect to that little boy that was on the inside of me. There were times when she would just need a hug and love. She had this thing she would do where she poked out her lip. It was a really cute baby look. LOL. It stole my heart every time. When she poked out that lip, I'd fall for whatever she wanted.

Tracey and I wanted two different things that neither one of us could be to the other at the time. As crazy as it sounds, I wanted her to be my mom, and she wanted me to man up and be her husband. There is a saying that goes, "When a woman loves, they love hard." I cannot say that is true for all women. I can say that Tracey really loved me with everything she had. Tracey loved me with her heart, body, and soul.

Needless to say, Tracey got to the point where she had had enough. She had had enough of the crying, the fighting, and my ways. She told me that she felt like she was in bondage. I felt like I was a dog on a leash. I felt sometimes like I could not be myself when I was with her. I agreed it did feel like we were in bondage.

In the early part of 2013, Tracey and I separated. She moved to Atlanta, Georgia, and then to Maryland with some old friends of ours. She came back home in April 2013 so we could sign the divorce papers. I really did not want to sign those papers. I did not want to lose her. I was the first one to arrive at the house where the divorce papers were gathered.

I walked into that house as if I were walking into the funeral of someone I knew. She walked in with her momma about ten minutes after I did. Man, she was looking so good, I had to turn my head the other way. That's when I knew I had really messed up. Tracey had a way of getting my attention. I think she dressed like that to show me what I would miss. I had not seen her since she left Jacksonville.

She sat by me as we signed the papers. The whole time I fought back tears. I wanted to flip the table over. I wanted to go off on her mom because I didn't understand the purpose of her being there. It felt like I was losing one thing that meant everything at one time. It felt like it was a tragedy.

That is what sin will do to an individual. It will appear to look good on the outside, but in the end, it'll keep you longer in darkness than what you want to be kept. It will make you pay more than what you expected to pay.

Tracey and I went through a lot of hell together, yes, but this woman knew everything about me. She knew all the right and wrong buttons to push. This woman knew exactly what to say to make me mad; she knew what hurt me the most. She knew what would make me light up like the lights on a Christmas tree. She loved me with a pure motherly love. The thought of that hurt the depth of my soul. I loved this girl, even though I had a hard time showing it.

I did not know how to be a husband, but I was trying based on what I saw with other married people. Tracey did not marry a man, she married a boy who wanted to be something that he did not know how to be. Every time things got hard, I ran, or I would go back to how I handled things when they got hard.

After we signed the divorce papers, I got in my car and sped off. The only thing on my mind was suicide. I mashed my foot down on the gas pedal and went from zero to eighty within seconds. I felt torn. I went home and sat down. I knew I was headed down the wrong path. I went through my phone and start deleting phone numbers and pictures of other women that I really liked. It hurt me to delete some of those pictures. It hurt so bad that I started crying.

I knew that God was telling me to do it.

On April 23, 2013, the divorce was settled. After the divorce, Tracey and I tried yet again to be a couple, but it didn't even last a week. A few weeks later, I called her and tried to talk to her. The conversation did not get anywhere. The way she was talking to me was as if I were a stranger or a waste of her time. That phone call ended by me throwing my phone across the room. On that day, I realized I still had some rage in me and that it was time to let it go.

Even though Tracey and I are divorced, I'm still certain that she has the love for me and I still have the love for her. I don't have anything bad to say about Tracey. I know that she is disgusted with my actions and the things I did. Yes, I've thought many times, *What if it was me in her shoes?* Honestly, I would be the same way. We all have flaws. We all need help. She is no better than me, and I'm no better than her. We grew up two different ways and struggled with different things.

My biggest hope is that Tracey will understand who I am. I was just a hurt boy expressing what was inside of me. I do wish the best for her. I know that she is going to excel in life. She is quiet but smarter than she looks, trust me.

As I close this part of my life, I want to say this section was not easy to write. To reread what I put Tracey through hurts, and I just wish I would've been what she wanted. However, I can't continue to be a prisoner of my past.

Tracey, I don't know when this book will reach you, but I'm pretty sure you will get ahold of it one day. I want to say thank you. Thank you for the love, support, and thank you for pushing me to do and be better. I will not quit.

Thoughts to Live By

Writing from my lens in 2013, the most valuable thing I have learned is that everything that I have gone through happened for a reason. It's a part of life's journey. What I went through wasn't for or about me, it was to help somebody else.

I made it out of foster care to let someone else know that they can make it out of the system, as well, with the help of God. I did not just make it out of foster care, I've made up my mind that I am going to be somebody with or without other people. It's nothing personal, that's just the mindset I created over the years. It may sound a little harsh, but that's just my reality.

Even though my marriage did not work, I'm grateful that I had that experience. My marriage showed me who I really was, the good and bad. I can now warn and help other people to not make the same mistakes that I did. I can also help someone else who may not understand what a marriage is all about.

That's what life is all about, helping and serving each other. It is not about accomplishing what is considered the "American Dream." The same principle applies to our lives. We were not created for ourselves. We were not created to get wealthy and rich for our own well-being or for our personal family. We were created to preach the gospel to the world and to be a servant to other people. We were created for God.

Five years later, in 2018, the same principle applies to my life. Life is a journey, and we should embrace it and go through the process. The sailing has not been smooth, but with the Heavenly Father as my guide, I am still on that path of striving to be the best version of myself and fulfill my purpose here on earth.

My childhood was not easy and one that I would not want for another child to go through, but from it all I have learned the importance of endurance, forgiveness, and self-fulfillment. My parents and I have forgiven each other, and while there is still room for improvements, one of my main drives in life is to ensure that I work at my relationship with my parents so that they can feel that I love them and have forgiven them for all that I have been through.

Also, I have forgiven myself and pray that anyone that I have hurt in the past has forgiven me. We all have one shot in life. This is not a mall or grocery store where you get to buy another life. You have only been given one, and after this life our earthly body will go back to where it came from: the ground. But, your soul on Judgement Day will be decided by God as to whether you will spend all eternity in Heaven or Hell. Choose this day the life you live and where you live after this life.

About the Author

Derrick L. Frazier is a driven, goal-oriented speaker and youth advocate who is passionate about what he does. His life is a testimony to the human spirit, and he uses his life journey to inspire others to be the best version of themselves. He lives by the gem "Embrace your journey and fall in love with the process."